MW00888321

THIRD EYE AWAKENING

Effective Techniques to Open Your Third Eye, Cleanse Your Pineal Gland, and Expand Awareness and Consciousness

ANNA MAI

TABLE OF CONTENT

INTRODUCTION

Thank you very much for your trust in purchasing this book. It should serve as a guide for your spiritual awakening. Step-by-step, you will learn effective techniques to quickly open your third eye by cleaning and decalcifying your pineal gland, thereby awakening your mind and consciousness.

Since ancient times, the third eye has been revered by various cultures as an organ of extrasensory perception, as a window to other dimensions, and as the seat of the soul – such cultures include the ancient mystery schools in ancient Egypt, the shamans in Tibet, the Celtic druids, and in Buddhism. Correspondingly, there are different designations. It is also known as the sixth chakra, ajna chakra (according to the Vedic tradition; ajna = to perceive), or forehead chakra, window of Brahma (Hinduism), eye of Horus (Egypt), third eye (China), Niwan Palace (Taoism), or seat of the soul (Descartes). It is also called the gateway to wisdom. It connects us with the spiritual world and lets us perceive things that are outside the usual perception of our senses.

Biologically, the third eye corresponds to the pineal gland. The German biophysicist Dieter Broers[1] calls it "the brain organ that makes us human". The pineal gland is the conductor; the main

---

1 https://dieterbroers.com/

rhythm generator which acts as a clock for all other glands and tunes them to each other, similar to a huge orchestra.

This tiny gland is the size of a grain of rice and located in the center of our brain. However, it is not responsible for our minds, but for the "higher molecules" - the higher states of being on the spiritual level, especially for the spiritual aspects of human beings.

It is the organ that reflects our inner wisdom and thus the ability to master all challenges in our everyday life by creating a connection between the body and the mind.

By opening the third eye, we can increase our cognitive ability and intuition, inner "vision" and clairvoyance, imagination and fantasy, empathy and wisdom, mental clarity and self-knowledge, memory, and extrasensory perception, as well as gain insight into higher realities beyond everyday consciousness. An awakened third eye also means to gain a feeling of love, awareness, knowledge, and compassion.

 The process of awakening begins with the decalcification of the pineal gland to open the ajna chakra. This prepares the way to connect with the universe or to connect your physical body with your soul.

The content of this book will help you to understand that we humans are all interconnected. There is nothing separating us, even if it often seems that way and especially when we think of people we don't like very much. However, this realization gives you the opportunity to let go of any negativities in your life. For some people, this may sound very esoteric at the beginning. Today, however, we are already able to physically prove these connections. Simply by sitting in a room with people in our immediate vicinity, we will still have a connection to these people after leaving the room. This connection can be proven for over a distance of 400 km, even if we did not verbally communicate with them.

The experiments at the European nuclear research center CERN, in which physicists succeeded in proving the interaction of protons shot in different directions over a long distance, are also exciting in this respect.

Take the time to read this book and understand how to open your mind and third eye. It is the gate to your freedom and I wish you much success!

1. WHAT DOES THE PINEAL GLAND ACTUALLY DO?

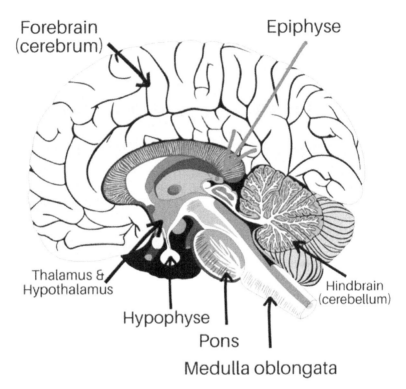

The pineal gland is a tiny organ in the brain which, despite its small physical size, has immense significance. It has diminished considerably in humans due to evolution and has shrunk from about three centimeters to just a few millimeters. This small gland is the shape of a pine cone and sits in the center of the brain, at the upper end of the brain stem between the two halves of the brain. It is exactly in the middle of the head and at the same level as the center of the eyebrows.

In humans, it has already developed in the prenatal state by the 7th week.

It has many different functions:

- It is the center of interaction between the right and left hemispheres of the brain.

- It is the clock for all other glands and many processes in the body.

- It converts the "happiness hormone" serotonin, produced during the day, into melatonin, which controls our inner clock and regulates the sleep-wake cycle. Melatonin is related to many other biological functions, such as kidney function and blood pressure.

- It controls sexual development.

- It protects against free radicals.

- It is of great importance for the immune system.

- It increases our intuition and imagination.

- It controls the hypothalamus.

- It controls the biorhythm.

- It is responsible for the release of DMT (N,N-Dimethyltryptamine), also called "The Spirit Molecule". This is the most powerful hallucinogenic neurotransmitter known; it is released during sleep when dreaming, meditating, and increasingly during near-death experiences. Near-death survivors often report of out-of-body perceptions and mystical visions.

- It is highly electromagnetically sensitive and also reacts to light, for example. Even blind people react to it.

- Due to its high density of magnetite crystals, it responds strongly to the earth's magnetic field with the corresponding psychological and spiritual effects.

Summary:

The pineal gland is extremely important for our physical, mental, and spiritual health. If it loses its function, physical and mental aging processes start.

2. WHAT DOES THE PINEAL GLAND HAVE TO DO WITH THE CHAKRA SYSTEM?

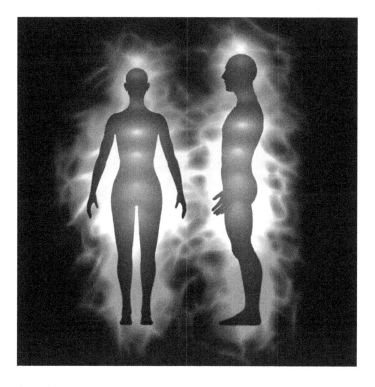

First, the pineal gland is a physical organ and part of the physical body. It is a part of the so-called aura, an energy field that penetrates and surrounds the human body.

The aura is invisible to most people, except for a few clairvoyant people who can perceive this field as a color spectrum. However, it can be made visible with so-called aura cameras[2]. It surrounds the physical body in an egg shape and has an extension of about half a meter around the body. The aura differs from person to person in

---

2 http://aurakamera.de/

color, structure, and form, depending on the state of mind and development of the person.

The aura is divided into several areas:

- The physical body is the area of the aura that vibrates at the lowest frequency. This is the area where energy has become matter.

- The next layer extends over the physical body and vibrates much faster than the physical body. This is called the etheric body. It is located up to about 10 cm above the skin and surrounds the person. In a way, it is the "mold" in which the physical body is formed.

- About 20 cm above the skin is the emotional body, which reflects and represents our feelings.

- About 30 cm above the skin is the mental body, which is related to our mental processes. The more our mind matches our feelings, the smoother its structure is.

- Between 30 and 50 cm above the skin is the so-called astral area. This represents the connection between the material and the immaterial plane and is divided into a (still material) astral body, a (bidirectional) mirror layer, and an (immaterial) astral plane. The entire astral realm is connected to our relationships.

- The further the individual layers are from the physical body, the faster they vibrate. From the immaterial astral plane onwards, the individual areas vibrate so highly and subtly that

10

one no longer speaks of "body" but only of "planes". Also on this immaterial plane is an etheric, an emotional, and a mental plane. The physical body is thus related to the immaterial planes which are mirrored by the bidirectional layer of the astral realm.

Within the aura there are energetic organs called chakras. The word chakra comes from Sanskrit and means "*spiral turning wheel*". These chakras are energy centers and gates to our levels of consciousness.

They open in a funnel shape out of the body and up to the astral region. They absorb energy and information and thus supply all energy bodies, including the physical body.

There are seven main chakras which are located on an axis close to the spine, starting from the crown chakra and down to the root chakra. This axis corresponds to the main energy channel and is called *Sushumna* in Sanskrit. The roots of the main chakras meet here in a balanced state.

The chakras are purely energetic and not physical. Nevertheless, they supply areas of the physical body with subtle energy and information. They are also connected to the endocrine glands of the physical body - including the pineal gland.

According to Indian yoga tradition, each chakra has certain tasks and is assigned to specific areas of life.

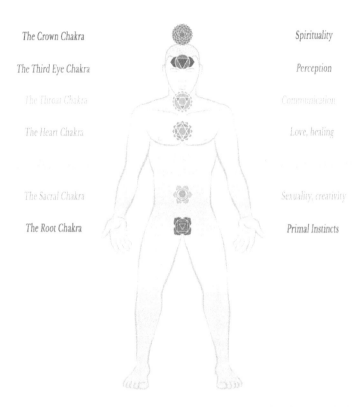

The Crown Chakra — Spirituality

The Third Eye Chakra — Perception

The Throat Chakra — Communication

The Heart Chakra — Love, healing

The Sacral Chakra — Sexuality, creativity

The Root Chakra — Primal Instincts

1. The root chakra (*muladhara chakra*) at the base of the spine provides for survival and primal instincts such as flight and fight.

2. The sacral or sexual chakra (*svadhisthana chakra*) at the level of the sacrum, near the pelvis, is responsible for sexuality and the preservation of the species. It is assigned to the reproductive organs and the male and female hormones.

3. The solar plexus chakra (*manipura chakra*) represents our own personality, the "I", as well as our own willpower and assertiveness. It is connected to the organs of metabolism, the pancreas. and the adrenal glands, among others.

4. The heart chakra (*anahata chakra*) in the middle of the chest at the heart level represents the transition between body and mind; between one's own personality and unity consciousness. It stands for a person's ability to connect and the goodness of their heart. It is assigned to the thymus gland (which controls the immune system), the heart organ, and the respiratory and vascular system, among other parts.

5. The throat chakra (vishudda chakra) at the level of the throat is connected to the thyroid gland, which - among other things - controls the physical and mental driving forces. It stands for all aspects of communication, self-expression, and expression.

6. The brow chakra (ajna chakra) is also called the third eye. This energy center is the command center for the pineal gland (epiphysis), the pituitary gland (hypophysis), and the hypothalamus. It is the control center for all hormones and the central nervous system. The hypothalamus controls functions such as body temperature, salt balance, all vegetative and endocrine processes, emotions, sleep, hunger, and thirst.

7. The crown chakra, also known as the sahasrara chakra, is located above the vertex or top of the head and is open upwards. According to the Indian yoga tradition, it connects man with the divine and cosmic. Through this connection, the highest form of wisdom can be attained. This is also summarized under the term "enlightenment".

Summary:

Chakras are energetic organs of the aura, the energy field that surrounds and penetrates the human being. According to the Indian yoga tradition, there are seven main chakras which are located along the spine. The sixth chakra, the so-called ajna chakra, is also called the third eye. It is connected to the pineal gland and its special functions.

3. WHAT ARE THE ADVANTAGES OF AN ACTIVATED PINEAL GLAND?

The pineal gland can do wonderful things for us, physically, mentally, and spiritually. However, this is only possible if it is intact and free of blockages of all kinds, whether they be poisoning, calcification, negative beliefs, or radiation. The pineal gland is our soul organ and is responsible for the expansion of consciousness, awareness, and wisdom. It enables us a better access to our intuitions, our fantasies, and our creativity. Only with an active pineal gland can we awaken our medial abilities, such as clairvoyance or clairsentience, and only with an intact pineal gland can the human body produce melatonin and from it the hallucinogen dimethyltryptamine (DMT).

From various studies[3] it is known that the melatonin production is very different in the life cycle of each person.

---

[3] http://warddeanmd.com/articles/neuroendocrine-theory-of-aging-chapter-2/

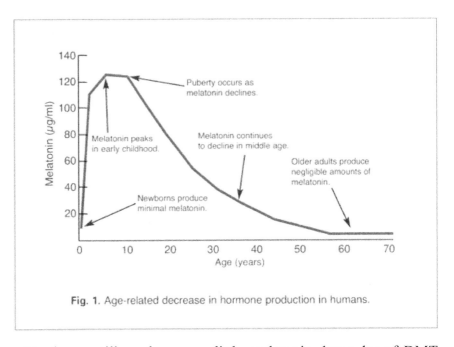

Fig. 1. Age-related decrease in hormone production in humans.

Newborns still produce very little melatonin, but a lot of DMT. Consequently, the brains of newborns and infants are still flooded with this hallucinogenic neurotransmitter. They are virtually still enlightened.

Then the melatonin level rises rapidly until the age of 15 and 16. Children have significantly higher melatonin levels than adults. However, the amount of melatonin in the blood level decreases drastically with increasing age. Starting from an age of 60 to 70 years, nearly no more melatonin is produced; this is often accompanied with sleep disorders at this age.

However, melatonin is much more than a hormone that controls the sleep rhythm; studies show other dramatic connections with melatonin deficiency. Thus, a connection can be made between a lack of melatonin and severe depression leading up to suicide, as well as other mental illnesses such as schizophrenia. This is supported by the discovery that depressive and schizophrenic patients show a significant melatonin deficiency.

Melatonin is also an anti-stress hormone[4], since so-called "stressors" (stress-inducing substances such as corticosteroids produced in the adrenal glands) can be controlled and destroyed.

Prof. Dr. Walter Pierpaoli from Switzerland and Italy and Dr. William Regelson from the USA, two of the most distinguished scientists in the field of age research, even call melatonin a "miracle hormone" or "immortality hormone" and the key to eternal youth, health, and fitness.[5] According to their research, melatonin is able to considerably slow down the aging process and prevent diseases such as cancer, Parkinson's, and Alzheimer's.

Melatonin can protect the DNA in the body's cells from changes caused by viruses and carcinogens (cancer-causing vectors) as well as strengthen the immune system. It is one of the most effective "antioxidants" and ensures the destruction of so-called "free radicals" (molecules with a free oxygen atom which cause damage to the cell membrane and can result in cancer).

---

4 http://warddeanmd.com/articles/neuroendocrine-theory-of-aging-chapter-2/

5 https://www.schallers-gesundheitsbriefe.de/archiv-der-gesundheitsbriefe/archiv-12/melatonin-schluessel-zu-ewiger-jugend-gesundheit-und-fitness-1/

Without the production of melatonin, no DMT can be produced. DMT is a hallucinogenic substance that also occurs in a variety of plants, fungi, and some animals.

In South America, the use of plants containing DMT and their preparation, such as ayahuasca or jurema with mimosa hostillis, is widespread - especially so in the context of shamanic ceremonies and in order to "think outside the box".

DMT plays a fundamental role in human consciousness. It is also known as the spirit molecule[6], which has the ability to lead us from one state of mind to another. During certain experiences, such as birth or near-death experiences, particularly high amounts of DMT are released. However, DMT also is released during the REM phases in which we dream every night when melatonin is produced. In these moments we gain access to our higher spheres. Unfortunately, we often cannot remember this when we wake up.

Nonetheless, there are ways to stimulate the release of DMT while we are awake - even without an artificial supply of DMT. More on this later.

Summary:

An active pineal gland has a significant impact on our physical, mental, and spiritual health. Only when it is active are melatonin and thus DMT produced. Therefore, maintaining health or activating the pineal gland is extremely important in several ways.

4. WHAT PREVENTS THE PINEAL GLAND FROM FUNCTIONING?

Through many of our daily habits, we poison, calcify, and radiate the pineal gland and prevent it from functioning.

Fluoride

Fluoride is a dangerous poison with a toxicity above that of lead and arsenic. Therefore, fluorides are also used in rat poison and insecticides.

Fluorides accumulate in the pineal gland, which is the highest concentration of fluoride in the human body. Fluoride causes small crystals to form in the pineal gland. As a result, it calcifies, becomes blocked, and consciousness cannot develop. Fluoride is therefore poison to this gland and can even cause it to close completely.

We find fluoride in drinking water, toothpaste, mouthwash, table salt, cosmetics, antibiotics, bread, processed meats, milk, chocolate, and some wines from the United States because their vines are often sprayed with fluoride-containing pesticides. Fluorides are also found in green and black tea.

High-dose fluoride gels are also commonly used for dental prophylaxis, which can give you more than one year's supply of fluoride within minutes. Even children and babies are administered fluoride to arm them against caries and tooth decay. Although fluoride has been officially recognized as a caries inhibitor for more than 20 years, not a single positive result has been achieved in caries prophylaxis to date. On the contrary, field studies could even show that in regions without fluorinated drinking water, far less caries occurred. In regions with fluorinated water, in contrast, dental fluorosis, the cancer rate, and osteoporosis increased.[7]

Fluoride is harmless in very small amounts. It also occurs naturally, but never pure; only in combination with other elements such as calcium and sodium.

However, the above mentioned products contain a fluoride that does not occur naturally and in a concentration that far exceeds the safety limit. In addition, the various fluoride additions which are often added to the body on a daily basis further compound this.

Another fluoride trap is the non-stick coated **Teflon**® pans with their three-layer fluoropolymer system. The perfluorinated surfactants (PTFE) used in their manufacture process are considered hazardous to the health by the European Food Safety Authority (EFSA). Nevertheless, Teflon pans may still be sold.

Teflon® is not only contained in pans, but is also used in fat-repellent pizza boxes, fast-food containers, popcorn bags for the microwave, packaging material for baked goods, beverages, and sweets, Gore-Tex, water-repellent clothing, dirt-repellent textiles, carpets, extinguishing foam, computer chips, and telephone cables.[8]

---

[7] https://www.zentrum-der-gesundheit.de/fluoridierung-ia.html
[8] https://www.zentrum-der-gesundheit.de/teflon-ia.html

Bromine

Bromine can also accumulate in the pineal gland, hardening and calcifying it. Bromine is an element that occurs naturally in many inorganic substances. Organic bromine, on the other hand, was released into the environment by humans and does not occur naturally. It is used in insect sprays, for example, but is not only harmful to insects; it also harms humans, who absorb it through their nose and skin. It damages the kidneys, lungs, spleen, nervous system, and gastrointestinal tract, in addition to altering the genetic material. Organic bromine is also used as a disinfectant and pesticide in greenhouses and on arable land, with fatal effects for animals and humans who ingest it through the food cycle.[9]

Calcium preparations

Calcium can only be processed by the body if sufficient vitamin D is available. Many humans suffer however from vitamin D deficiency, e.g. office workers, the elders in nursing homes etc.

Therefore, it is important to be careful when using artificial calcium supplements such as di-calcium phosphate, calcium carbonate, and calcium phosphate. These are contributory causes of pineal calcification. If a calcium deficiency is present, natural sources of calcium are more useful, such as broccoli, oranges, quinoa, cabbage, spinach, chia seeds, and sesame seeds.

Mercury

---

[9] https://www.lenntech.de/pse/elemente/br.htm

Mercury is one of the heaviest and most toxic metals, being even more toxic than radioactive metals. It causes serious brain damage including damage to the pineal gland. Many vaccines are alleged to contain mercury. This is especially dangerous when young children are already vaccinated and sometimes have to be vaccinated up to 8 times before their immune system has developed, meaning their pineal gland cannot develop at all because it has been blocked from the beginning. Some versions of the influenza vaccine also contain mercury, so the question of whether this vaccination makes sense should be investigated and answered by everyone.

Dental fillings, especially those made of amalgam, also contain mercury and lead to the calcification of the pineal gland. Amalgam releases small amounts of toxic mercury and its consequences include headaches, psychological changes, concentration problems, poor memory, depression, and persistent states of exhaustion. [10]

Caution is also required when eating fish. Fish is generally considered healthy. However, it should be noted that the limit value of mercury for certain types of fish has now been raised so that they can still be sold in stores despite their high mercury content. These include swordfish, tuna, perch, pike, mackerel, sturgeon, halibut, redfish, cod, and monkfish. The origin of the fish naturally has a

---

10 „... Many tons of toxic mercury are consumed per year for amalgam fillings in the teeth ... Dentists and assistants are extremely endangered by handling amalgam. .... The life expectancy of dentists is the lowest compared to other professional groups". http://www.zahnheilkunde-uelzen.de/amalgam.html

great influence on their mercury content; the least contaminated are fish from large oceans.

Pesticides

Pesticides such as Roundup (glyphosate) are highly toxic and significantly contribute to pineal calcification. You can find them in food, water, and the environment.

Other toxins

Artificial sweeteners such as aspartame, sucralose, and saccharin, room scents with synthetic fragrances, chemical detergents, deodorants, products with E-numbers, and phyleneanines are also substances that poison and block the pineal gland. Furthermore, the numerous toxins in tobacco, alcohol, caffeine, and sugar, which can be found in almost every processed food, can trigger pineal calcification.

Sleep rhythm and artificial light

A healthy sleep rhythm is required for the production of melatonin. Since the pineal gland works synchronously with the 24-hour cycle of the world revolution, it is important to achieve a natural day/night cycle. Those who frequently work at night and use artificial light, especially the blue light emitted by computers, prevent the pineal gland from functioning properly.

Electrosmog

Even what we cannot see with our eyes can damage us.

"An ever-increasing number of scientific studies prove that the greatest threat to our health (and that of all life forms) currently emanates from the creeping, omnipresent and invisible pollution of our environment, which is called electrosmog. [11]

Many health problems are associated with EMR (Electromagnetic Radiation), including some types of cancer (especially tumors in the brain, eye, or ear and leukemia), miscarriages, malformations, chronic fatigue, headaches, stress, dizziness, heart problems, autism, learning difficulties, insomnia, and Alzheimer's. The impairment of our hormonal balance is perhaps one of the most worrying effects of EMR. Needless to say, it is important for the body to produce adequate amounts of melatonin every day. Unfortunately, sleeping in a room that contains all our beloved devices - wireless phones, cell phones, digital watches, CD players, radios, computers, and TVs - can severely inhibit our nightly production of melatonin. It is believed that electromagnetic radiation unfolds its harmful side effects in this very way.

Cell phone waves[12], Wi-Fi (Wireless Local Area Network), satellites, pulsed microwaves from mobile phone transmitters, microwave ovens, cell phone masts, multiple sockets, DECT (Digital

---

[11] https://www.nexus-magazin.de/artikel/lesen/elektrosmog-und-hormonstoerungen

[12] Statements of the physicist Prof. Dr. Konstantin Meyl on mobile radio, https://www.youtube.com/watch?v=IwMoPyQiQV8

Enhanced Cordless Telecommunications-) cordless phones, etc. are all left-polarized electromagnetic fields. These fields run in the exact opposite direction to our natural energy field, which has clockwise rotating properties except for the intestine. Left-turning fields draw energy from the body and cause great damage to the pineal gland.

Do not underestimate the radiation of headsets with their highly dangerous Bluetooth technology. According to the Institute for Environmental Analysis[13] *"... hands-free car kits keep your hands free. But they do not protect against radiation. On the contrary: They conduct the electrosmog from the cell phone directly into the ear. All hands-free sets absorb the radiation of the cell phone antenna and conduct it to the ear. Pulsed microwaves are held responsible by critical medical experts for a number of effects in the body - such as changes in brain waves, headaches, nervousness and insomnia. That is why hands-free devices, which conduct the radiation directly to the head, are not recommended"*.

Stress, exhaustion, and lack of spiritual practice

Through too much stress, the chakras become blocked. Those who are under constant pressure and do not take the time to meditate or partake in spiritual practices from time to time will eventually block their pineal gland. It is like a muscle that needs to be trained occasionally.

---

[13] http://www.umweltanalytik.com/ing104.htm

Summary:

These factors significantly affect the functions of the pineal gland:

- Fluoride (tap water, toothpaste, mouthwash, table salt, cosmetics, antibiotics, bread, processed meats, milk, chocolate, Teflon pans, fat-repellent pizza boxes, fast food containers, popcorn bags, packaging material for baked goods, drinks, and sweets, Gore-Tex, carpets, fire-fighting foam, computer chips, and telephone cables)
  - Bromine (insect sprays, disinfectants, and plant protection products)
  - Mercury (vaccinations, amalgam, fish)
  - Potassium preparations as food supplements
  - Pesticides
  - Artificial sweeteners
  - Room fragrances with synthetic scents
  - Chemical cleaning agents
  - Deodorants
  - Products with E-numbers and phyleneanines
  - Tobacco, alcohol, caffeine, sugar
  - Processed food
  - Unhealthy sleep rhythm (artificial light, blue computer light)
  - Electrosmog (WLAN, cell phone, DECT, Bluetooth, etc.)
  - Stress and a lack of spiritual practice

5. How can I determine if my pineal gland is working?

To determine if your pineal gland is still intact and functioning, read the following statements. The more statements that apply to you, the more likely your pineal gland is still intact:

- It does not bother you to meditate.

- You can remember your dreams well.

- You do not feel lost or separated from the source.

- When you close your eyes, it is easy to visualize colors. To imagine something vividly, you need the activity of the pineal gland.

- You have no problems sleeping. A healthy sleep-wake rhythm is the prerequisite for the pineal gland to function.

- You are creative and well concentrated.

- You can easily remember the last time you were full of happiness and joy.

- You are not depressed and feel your inner power.

- You are a rather patient person.

- You rarely forget anything.

- You are not superstitious.

- You rarely blame the behavior of your fellow men.

- You do not feel excluded.

- You seldom worry, are not anxious, and trust in life.

- You do not doubt yourself or others.

- You feel in harmony with and love your surroundings.

If you could affirm most of these statements, then your pineal gland seems to still be intact. If not, then there is the possibility that it is already calcified. Thus, you should clean it and activate it. I will show you the possibilities for this in the following chapter.

6. How can I open my third eye?

The process of opening the third eye begins with the cleaning and activation of the pineal gland. This enables you to open your energetic center for wisdom, insight, intuition, perception, imagination, and self-knowledge. Afterwards it is important to avoid further calcification.

This, of course, includes a change in diet and lifestyle which should definitely be part of your program. Furthermore, I will introduce you to other highly effective instruments and techniques to accelerate the process of activation.

There are many ways to open the third eye. Take one or the other path, or choose a combination of them. It is up to you. In the end, it is the practice that makes the master and decides how successful you are.

6.1 METHODS FOR CLEANSING

First of all, it is important to dissolve the fluorides and other pollutants that have accumulated in the pineal gland over the years. The decomposition of the lime capsule around the pineal gland can be supported by various fish oils, microalgae, coconut, and cedar nut oil, as well as numerous other means. As soon as the lime is dissolved, the fluoride it contains can dissolve.

Here I will introduce you to an energetic method to cleanse your pineal gland. This is one of the fastest and most effective methods. You will also learn about a variety of other methods that physically cleanse the pineal gland of harmful substances. Furthermore, you can combine these methods if you so wish.

ENERGETIC CLEANSING VIA NUMERICAL CODES

The method of healing using numerical codes was developed by the Russian clairvoyant, healer, and specialist in energy informatics Grigori Grabovoi. It works purely on the mental level - or rather on the subconscious. Only through our subconscious can our own body be induced to regenerate and heal itself without any aids.

Grabovoi developed unique combinations of numbers and numerous other spiritual methods to restore health. He showed how everyone was able to heal themselves from all kinds of illnesses and, as a creator, control all events of their reality. This concerns both the general living conditions and improvement of the financial flow up to the expansion of consciousness and spiritual growth. Everything can be returned to the original order. These numerical codes always work.

For mathematicians, this healing method according to number codes is not so far off the mark. Everything in and around us is built according to number systems. Even music, colors, and sounds are ultimately systems of vibrations and numbers.

The numerical code for draining fluoride from the pineal gland and your body is:

16218391499

There are different ways to let this code affect your body. Choose something that feels good for you and repeat it several times a day for a few days.

- Write the code on a piece of paper and put it under a glass of water for at least 11 minutes. Drink the water within the next 2 hours.

- Put the code directly on your forehead while you take a nap.

- Just carry the code with you, e.g. in your jacket pocket.

- Visualize the code in front of your inner eyes by painting it in your mind with huge numbers in the air. Breathe out everything that disturbs you.

- Write the code on a body part.

ACTIVATOR X

The name "Activator X"[14] goes back to research by the dentist Dr. Weston Price from Cleveland, USA. Also known as the "Isaac Newton of Nutrition", he was a scientist and dentist of the early 20th century. Activator X not only has numerous positive effects on dental health, but also helps to decalcify the pineal gland, detoxify heavy metals such as mercury, and promote concentration.

Ultimately, it is vitamin K2 or the isoform MK-4 (menatetrenone). To date, however, it is not known which active ingredient is crucial in the decalcification of the pineal gland, whether it be K2 or MK4.

Activator X can be found at a high percentage in various fish oils (e.g. ray cod liver oil, cod liver oil, or sea cats liver oil).

Application:

Fish oils are more effective in liquid form than in capsule form, but should always be kept in the refrigerator. The daily dose is 20 drops per day. After that, 1-5 milliliters per day are sufficient for general health maintenance. In order to achieve significant effects, it is recommended to take the oil over a period of about 3 months.

---

14 American scientist and dentist Weston Price was horrified by the poor dental condition of his patients and examined several so-called "primitive peoples" who obviously had no dental problems and were much healthier and more robust than "city dwellers.
He came to the following conclusion: regardless of their ethnic origin, their food always contained three fat-soluble vitamins: vitamin A, vitamin D and a substance whose chemical structure he could not decipher in more detail. He called this "Activator X". He found "Activator X" in high concentrations in the milk or butter of grass-fed cows. Also in insects, oils from chimeras (sea cats, sea rats), certain fish eggs, shellfish, crabs and in the meat of poultry. With the help of this Activator X, he was able to treat his dental patients with great success. He documented the positive results with X-ray images. Unfortunately, his discoveries in the public received little attention for a long time.

RAW COCOA

Due to its highly concentrated antioxidants, raw cocoa (not chocolate!) detoxifies and stimulates the pineal gland simultaneously. Cocoa beans can only develop their full effect in raw form if they are not heated above 42° Celsius. By adding sugar and milk, the healing effect of the cocoa bean is destroyed and the cocoa bean's antioxidants are blocked. Only in its raw state does cocoa have 30 times more antioxidants than green tea.

CITRIC ACID

Citric acid and organic lemons also have a positive effect on decalcification.

Application:

3 teaspoons of citric acid daily or seven organic lemons before meals for two to three weeks. Mix it with good spring water or mineral water.

GARLIC

Garlic contributes to detoxification by dissolving calcium. It also acts as an antibiotic and strengthens the immune system.

Directions for use:

Use half a clove of garlic chopped into fresh lemon juice or soaked in apple cider vinegar daily. Black garlic is particularly effective.

RAW CIDER VINEGAR

Raw cider vinegar contains malic acid and decalcifies the entire body.

Application:

Use cider vinegar only from glass bottles and not from plastic bottles. You can dilute it with some water or use it as a dressing.

NEEM TREE EXTRACT

The Neem tree has been known to be a medicinal plant for a long time and plays an important role in Ayurvedic medicine. It was mentioned in old Sanskrit writings and its ingredients have many positive effects. They are fungicidal, virucidal, insecticidal, pesticidal, anti-inflammatory, and an excellent antibiotic.

Application:

When taking Neem tree extract, always follow the respective recommendations. Never take it on an empty stomach.

OREGANO OIL

Oregano is one of the most powerful herbs with effective natural antibiotics. Oregano oil is also effective against all kinds of fungal infections, resistant against bacteria and intestinal parasites, and is ideally suited to support the organism in detoxification.

Directions for use:

Add oregano oil to a glass of water (1 to 5 drops per glass).

BORAX (SODIUM BORATE)

Borax contains the essential elements boric acid and boron. It helps to flush out the released fluoride from the body. It also dissolves lime and helps to eliminate fluoride from the body.

Directions for use:

300 mg of borax for one liter of low fluoride mineral water. No more under any circumstances! Additionally, use a pinch of fluoride-free rock salt. Shake the mixture well and drink it throughout the day. You can also make yourself a tea with the mixture.

If the mixture is too strong for you, weaken it. After 5 days, take a 2-day break so that your body can calm down again. You may experience mild kidney pain or tension, head pressure, or slight dizziness as the fluoride is released and sent through the bloodstream. This is part of the healing process and not a cause for concern.

IODINE

Clinical tests have shown that iodine can enhance fluoride degradation via urine. Our diet is usually low in iodine because it contains little sea fish. However, you should not use artificially iodized salt to absorb iodine, but should resort to sea vegetables such as Dulse or Arame algae or Hijiki algae.

Note: A detoxification of fluoride with iodine has the disadvantage that valuable calcium is removed from the body. Therefore, it is better to resort to a natural calcium-iodine-magnesium source, such as Sango Sea Coral with a natural blend of essential minerals from the sea.

TAMARIND

The leaves of the tamarind tree are helpful for fluoride elimination. You can prepare extracts or a tea from them. You can buy tamarind leaves in such places as Asian grocery stores. Tamarind leaves have other health benefits besides detoxifying the pineal gland. Paracelsus, pioneer of modern medicine and pharmacology, mentioned tamarind as a remedy for fever, headaches, stomach disorders, and much more.

MELATONIN

In American naturopathy, melatonin is used to remove fluorides from the body and to decalcify the pineal gland. In some countries, melatonin is not freely available and is only exceptionally prescribed as a remedy for jet lag.

Note: The precursor of melatonin is L-tryptophan. Tryptophan is an essential amino acid/protein building block and the precursor of serotonin and melatonin. L-tryptophan is approved as a dietary supplement in many countries.

BLACK CUMIN OIL

Black caraway has its origin in western Asia. It supports the immune system, acts as an antibacterial, antihistamine, and anti-inflammatory, and is helpful in pineal decalcification.

Application:

1 tablespoon of high-quality cold-pressed black cumin oil daily.

ZEOLITE AND BENTONITE

Bentonite and zeolite are healing and mineral soils that can bind toxins strongly, so that the bound toxins can be excreted quickly through the intestines. Due to their high absorption power, they are ideal for internal use. They also offer effective protection against radioactivity and radioactive elements, promoting the elimination of mercury from the organism.

CHAGA MUSHROOMS

Chaga mushrooms are the most powerful antioxidant in the world. They act as an anti-inflammatory and antibacterial in viral diseases and stimulates the killer cells of the immune system. They also support decalcification.

Application:

- Tea: brew 3-4 small pieces of dried mushrooms (about 10 g) with hot water and drink 1 to 5 cups daily.

- Chaga powder: with coffee or as a coffee substitute.

MICROALGAE

The micro algae Spirulina, Chlorella, or AFA (Aphanizomenon flos-aquae) Blue-Green Algae contribute to the detoxification of the entire body.

- Spirulina and Chlorella: These microalgae provide a high dose of essential amino acids, valuable vitamins, minerals, and trace elements. Chlorella can also bind and eliminate free toxins, especially metals, to an even greater extent than spirulina. It is therefore particularly recommended for the healing and regeneration process.

- AFA Blue-Green Algae: This is a wild plant from Lake Klamath in Oregon/USA, which lies 1400 meters above sea level. Since it grows wild, it has an even higher biopotential than Spirulina and Chlorella. It has a special effect on the brain, ensures clear thoughts, increases concentration, and discharges heavy metals - especially from the brain. It also contains the special mineral germanium, which is not found in chlorella and spirulina. Germanium has a strong effect on the pineal and pituitary glands and the higher chakras associated with them. To achieve the same concentration of ingredients, one would have to consume 3 to 4 times the amount of spirulina and chlorella.

Note: To cleanse the pineal gland, the AFA algae is highly recommended.

COCONUT OIL AND CEDAR NUT OIL

Coconut oil helps detoxify the body and rid the pineal gland of fluorides and other deposits.

The same applies to cedar nut oil, which is obtained from the nuts of the Siberian pine. One of the best is cedar nut oil, according to Anastasia from the Siberian taiga. The product is called "The Sounding Cedars of Russia"[15]). It is superior to other oils in both quality and effect.

Application:

Add 1 teaspoon of the respective oil to a meal.

---

[15] https://www.sibirische-zedernprodukte.com/zedernprodukte/zedernussoel-nach-anastasia/392/zedernussoel-mit-10-harz-von-fa.megre

6.2 METHODS FOR ACTIVATING THE PINEAL GLAND

For most people, the pineal gland simply performs its biological function of controlling the sleep-wake cycle. However it is capable of much more, as we now know. For this purpose, it is important that it can fulfill its full functionality and allow you to experience higher spiritual awareness, more developed intuition, and expanded mental and intellectual visions.

6.2.1. MEDITATION

The most effective and best method to activate the pineal gland is meditation, meditation, and meditation again. This is also obvious. After all, it is about a spiritual goal - namely the expansion of consciousness. For this, it is necessary to be calm, to listen to oneself, or to perceive one's inner voice, emotions, and intuitions. Those who only work through their to-do lists every day - living in the stress of everyday life and believing that, if they can reach higher mental and spiritual abilities with the appropriate tools, they will suddenly attain magical powers - will be more likely to be disappointed. There isn't really a shortcut, only one or the other form of support through sounds, essential oils, or crystals.

Entering a deep meditation state and focusing all your energy on the third eye chakra can be a very powerful way to activate the pineal gland. It takes a lot of practice and concentration, but it´s the best way to activate your third eye. I can recommend the detailed guided powerful meditation guide of "Holo Vibe". It activates the pineal body and opens the third eye, as well as awakening the sixth sense. Doing this meditation for 3 weeks guarantee that your third eye will open.

More infos on YouTube: "Instantly Awaken Your Energetic Sense and Activate your Pineal Gland" ... https://youtu.be/xg1VLjqowkE

The best time to practice the third eye activation and spiritual practices is right after you wake up, because your brain is still in theta wave status. Instead of getting out of your bed, lie still and focus on your intention of opening your third eye. The more you are training to open the third eye to see beyond the material world, the stronger it gets. As your pineal gland becomes more active, the ability to access to high wave energies becomes increasingly easier.

In the following, I will show you a meditation that is well-suited for the activation of the third eye. Please adapt it to your personal preferences.

Meditation instructions:

- Choose a quiet place where you are undisturbed. Minimize the electromagnetic fields in your environment, be it through Wi-Fi routers, smartphones, or multiple power outlets. If possible, it's best to meditate outside, e.g. on the grass, on the sand of a beach, on stones, or on other natural ground.

- Wear comfortable clothing and sit upright on a yoga mat or chair. Tense your abdominal muscles to support the upper body.

- Move your head slowly from side to side a few times to relax the neck.

- Close your eyes and take three deep breaths, in and out.

- With the next breath, imagine golden light flowing into your body and expanding like a golden sea. Say the word "light" inwardly.

- As you exhale, imagine how dark energies or emotions leave your body.

- Repeat the inhalation and exhalation in this way at least twelve times.

- Direct the attention to your forehead and imagine a round golden light in front of it, about 15 cm in diameter. The light rotates and floats like a wind.

- Imagine the light slowly opening and flowing directly into your third eye, activating it.

- Keep breathing calmly. Relax and let the light move into your forehead. Keep the focus on your third eye for 10 to 15 minutes. If disturbing thoughts occur, imagine a transparent wiper that pushes the thoughts aside.

- Take your left hand and gently touch your forehead. Feel how the light penetrates through the palm of your hand, into your brow chakra.

- When you get a feeling for your third eye and feel that you have activated it enough, take your hand away again.

- Take three deep breaths, in and out, trying to imagine the golden light in your mind.

- Then, slowly open your eyes again and sit for another 3 to 4 minutes with relaxed eyes. Concentrate on what you have experienced. Enjoy the peace and silence in your body and feel into yourself, your head and your soul.

This meditation not only clears your head, but also lets your inner sun shine again. The more often you meditate, the more you notice how your third eye becomes more active. It is normal to feel warmth in the area of the pineal gland when you meditate. If the heat becomes too intense, it is a sign that you are on your way to a deeper spirituality. If it irritates you too much, then interrupt the meditation and continue it the next day. Give yourself the time you need to follow your spiritual path.

Sometimes the third eye opens suddenly, without intention or planning, and you find yourself at a much higher level of intuition. This happens especially after a near-death experience, before or after the loss of a loved one, after the birth of a child, or after a session of energetic healing like Reiki or hypnosis.

6.2.2. JOY

During the cleansing of the chakras, their blockages and disorders are removed so that the life energy can once again flow unhindered, meaning more energy is available again. Through the increase in energy, your own vibrations also increase. This in turn leads to an expanded consciousness. The higher our body vibrates, the happier we are. The highest vibrational state we can reach as human beings is unconditional love. Maybe you know of this state or moment, if you have already been completely in love.

Before we wait for an increase in vibration from outside sources, there are many preliminary stages to tackle. One of them is joy. Thus, instead of waiting until you are in a state of unconditional love, we can go into a state of joy. Joy in this sense does not mean the little material happiness we get through consumption, but rather a joy of an immaterial kind. The joy of a beautiful sunset, of the fascination of nature, of new knowledge, of the health and laughter of your children. By the way, children are good role models here!

An active pineal gland is directly connected to the energy of the heart. Therefore, whether in meditation or in everyday life, try to perceive and feel feelings of joy more intensely. Even if many things in this world don't work out the way you want them to, you are not doing yourself or this world any favors when you walk through life full of anger and rage. After all, with this you do not change anything and only bring yourself to a low vibration level. It is better to create the reality you wish to live for yourself. With your vibrations, you can create the reality you want.

It is often said that our thoughts create our reality, but rather it is our feelings. Only that which you can feel is energy and determines and defines your world, your mood, and your attitude. Therefore, our feelings are our most powerful tool. They guide you to your healing.

So come back to your feelings. They are the strongest drive and the most powerful expression of life.

A little exercise should help you to get back into the state of joy:

- Sit relaxed on a yoga mat or chair and close your eyes.
- Remember a moment in your past when you were completely happy and full of joy or love. Wait until you have found such a moment, even if it may be far in the past.
- With every breath, breathe this joy into yourself.

- Become aware that the past does not exist. Only the present - the now - exists.

- Imagine how filling a small bright cloud hovering above you with this joy. With every breath, it becomes bigger and bigger. At the same time, the state of your joy and love increases.

- Visualize how you send the cloud on a journey towards the earth, which you observe from far away. You send it to all animals and to all people - and thus also to you.

Repeat this exercise again and again to bring yourself into a higher spiritual vibration and, thus, into a state of joy and love. Even if you can't always avoid it, spend less and less time with things that make you suffer, meaning you find a good balance between things that feel good for you and things that frighten or annoy you.

6.2.3. SOUNDS

"If you want to discover the secrets of the universe, think in terms of energy, frequency and vibration." Nikola Tesla

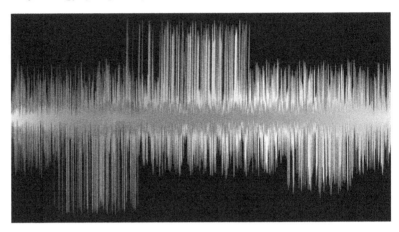

Frequencies of music and sounds have a powerful effect on our consciousness. Indian mantras also remind us of the effect of sounds on the mind and body. We can all consciously let their effect flow into our lives and profit from it. They are the connecting links between scientifically-provable and intentionally-experienced qualities of human consciousness.

Every part of the body, every organ, all cells, all systems in our body vibrate with certain frequencies. The pineal gland itself has a frequency of 8 Hz.

Sounds are also vibrations. Through sounds, we can influence our body in a healing way.

Here I present three different healing sounds or sound patterns. They are all suitable to activate the pineal gland. You will achieve the greatest benefit from them in connection with meditation.

6.2.3.1 BINAURAL BEATS

Binaural beats are an acoustic method to influence brain waves via the neural system. They are sounds that are produced in the brain when two frequencies, each slightly different, are played simultaneously. This results in a difference between the sounds which is also called *beat frequencies*. However, this only occurs when the frequency difference is below 30 Hz. If the differences were greater, the ear would notice the crooked sound.

Binaural beats have been scientifically researched for over 100 years and the results they produce are not considered the placebo effect. So far, no side effects have been observed except for headaches or short-term dizziness. They are used for neurological programming during which the hemispheres are synchronized and brought into an even structure.

Binaural beats are used for various purposes, like increasing self-esteem, concentration, creativity, and the ability to learn, improving vision, sleep, and hair growth, and shielding against allergies, depression, anti-aging, and much more. They are also suitable to influence the pineal gland. As already described, it oscillates with a frequency of 8 Hz which can be triggered by binaural sounds.

CDs and/or mp3s with binaural beats can be found on the Internet (for example https://www.gehirnkicker.de/dilas-gehirnkick/). Consciousness researcher Jonathan Dilas presents different music tracks under which binaural beats are mixed in order to induce the desired condition in each case.

6.2.3.2 SOLFEGGIO SOUNDS

Different scales have developed all over the world. Normally a scale is comprised of one octave and repeats itself with double frequency. There are scales that contain 5 or even 12 tones. In the Gregorian churches of the Middle Ages, however, a scale containing 6 tones was used - the so-called six-tone scale. These tones are based on the so-called solfeggio frequencies which are said to have a particularly healing effect on humans.

Solfeggio comes from the Italian language and is derived from the note syllables "Sol" and "Fa". It was originally a singing exercise practiced by the monk Guido of Arezzo in the 11th century and used to train the singing of the monastery boys in order to speed up the training. For reasons still unknown today, the church decided at that time to stop using music with these frequencies in church services and replace it with other pieces of music.

The knowledge about this special scale and its frequencies was not passed on for a long time. Moreover, for centuries people were denied access to these special frequencies by the church. One can only speculate about the reasons; perhaps the church did not want people to find their salvation and be happy without desire. It was not until 1999 that the knowledge of the Solfeggio sounds was made available to the wider public again by the US-American researcher Leonard G. Horowitz.

The frequency 528 Hz has a special meaning- it is also called "Mi" by the Italian term Mira (miracle).

The following are the sound frequencies of the six-tone scale which have a certain effect on human consciousness:

- The frequency 396 Hz ("UT"queant laxis = to solve) is said to dissolve guilt and fear.

- The frequency 417 Hz ("Re"sonare fibris = echo fibers) facilitates changes and has a mind-expanding effect.

- The frequency 528 Hz ("MI"ra gestorum = wonderful deeds) is used by scientists today to heal defective DNA strands.

- The frequency 639 Hz ("FA"muli tuorum = your servants) promotes connections and the ability to relate.

- The frequency 741 Hz ("SOL"ve polluti = lose the worldly) awakens the intuition.

- The frequency 852 Hz ("LA"bii reatum = colorful/spotted lips) promotes spiritual development.

Other important Solfeggio frequencies are:

- The frequency 174 Hz: for grounding and pain relief.

- The frequency 285 Hz: for visualization and manifestation of thoughts.

- The frequency 939 Hz: for stimulating the pineal gland via the so-called Corti organ. This is the interface between acoustic vibrations and the nerve signals in the inner ear.[16]

Summary:

Solfeggio frequencies have a healing effect on humans.

The frequency 939 Hz stimulates the pineal gland. The effect of meditation to open the third eye can be amplified by this sound.

---

[16] A sound sample of the connection of the 939 Hz frequency with the binaural beats can be found on YouTube: https://youtu.be/3h2mJnvRbZ8 *"936Hz Activation of the Pineal Gland Solfeggio of the Meditation Gland with Binaural Frequencies"*

6.2.3.3 SOUND COMPOSITION AUMEGA

The sound composition auMega[17] by the German biophysicist Dieter Broers[18] offers a similar approach. This project is based on scientifically sound findings. It uses the phenomenon of sound as the basis and connection between scientifically proven and consciously experienced qualities of human consciousness. Through sound compositions you can put yourself in a meditation-like state and move from everyday consciousness to the lowest frequencies of your brain wave activity. In this way, your mind can be calmed and a state of absolute peace and balance can be achieved to support your holistic personal growth.[19]

The scientific basis of the sound architecture has been developed by Dieter Broers. The compositions are by the Austrian sound designer Thomas Chochola.

---

[17] https://shop.dieterbroers.com/produkt/aumega-download/
[18] https://dieterbroers.com/
[19] With the auMega compositions, „... *among other things, prime number series in the form of polyrhythmic pulsations, tempered as well as purely tuned cluster chords with natural sounds and result in an exogenous sound structure, which offers the body's own rhythms a return to a holistic awareness. During this interaction resonance phenomena can occur, which can be interpreted as solution processes of accumulated conditioning patterns.*" *Dieter Broers*

6.2.4. VIBRATION EXERCISES

Instead of using external sounds, you can also create vibrations yourself. Here I present three exercises with which you can stimulate your pineal gland directly and relatively quickly.

Exercise 1

- Sit down and make sure that your back is straight.

- Hold your hands over your ears.

- Close your mouth and press your tongue lightly against your front palate and create the sound "nnnnnnnn". Hold it for a few minutes (with interruptions, of course, to catch your breath). You will feel the vibrations in your head.

- Then create the sound "mmmmmm" for a few minutes by pressing your lips together slightly.

- Then create the sound "ngngngngng" in your throat for a few minutes.

This is a very simple method of activation. The vibrations you create stimulate and activate your pineal gland.

Exercise 2

This exercise can also be mastered in a short time.

- Open your jaw slightly; place your tongue between the upper and lower jaw so that the teeth rest easily on the tongue, similar to the pronunciation of the English "th".

- Breathe in and fill your lungs with air.

- When exhaling, make a sound in a medium natural pitch. Press the air through the slightly open mouth while the tongue remains relaxed between the upper and lower jaw. The air moves very quickly between the teeth and tongue. Your tongue, jaws, and cheeks will start to vibrate.

- Now try to open the throat at the back at the same time so that you don't create a "The", but a "Thooooo". It may take a little practice to simultaneously get the tongue vibrating between the teeth at the front with an open O at the back of the throat. This vibration has a direct effect on the pineal gland, stimulating and activating it.

- Repeat the exercise five times in a row. Then repeat this vibration exercise for 3 consecutive days. There should be 24 hours left between each exercise session.

- Then take a 10- to 14-day break before starting with exercise 3, meaning that the activation and stimulation of the third eye can slowly adjust.

Note: If you feel any pressure or pain in the middle of your head during the exercise process, there is no need to worry. This means that your third eye is waking up. You may also experience a tingling or throbbing sensation in your forehead when you wake up. It can sometimes become more intense, as if a sound seems to be coming from inside your head. This is also a positive sign that your third eye is waking up.

Exercise 3

- Take a deep breath through your nose and hold it while you count to five. Exhale slowly. Repeat this 3 times so that you feel well relaxed.

- Focus your concentration on your third eye in the middle of your brain.

- Take a very deep breath again and hold it for as long as possible.

- Now exhale slowly while pronouncing the vibrating word "May" like a long M-a-a-a-a-a-a-a-i. Again, use a medium natural pitch while pronouncing the word.

- Wander with your concentration as you exhale from your third eye, in the middle of your head, to your vertex chakra, above the vertex. The exhalation should take place in a single flow.

- Repeat this exercise 5 times.

Note: The effect of this exercise is very pleasant. When performed correctly, a flow of energy can be felt in the body which is sometimes combined with a feeling of lightness. Some people also feel a tingling sensation in the head or a slight pressure in the area of the crown chakra. Euphoric feelings are also common, including a blissful state that lasts for hours or even days.

6.2.5. SUNGAZING

The sun supplies all of our body's cells with energy. So, all over the world people are discovering so-called sungazing and connecting with the sun, the direct source that drives all life.

Sungazing is an ancient healing method that dates back to ancient India and over 2000 years ago. It helps to get better sleep, gain energy, relieve pain, improve perception, strengthen the hormone balance, expand consciousness, and decalcify and activate the pineal gland.

Sungazing also has the effect of enriching the body with vitamin D and vitamin A. Vitamin A is important for the health of the eyes. If you use sungazing for a while, you will also see better again – you may even be able to do so without glasses.

Sungazing involves looking directly into the rising or setting sun once a day. The safe times are in the one-hour window after sunrise or before sunset. It is scientifically proven that at these times the content of UV radiation is at its lowest and our eyes suffer little to no damage.

Take the exact times of sunrise and sunset from your local newspaper and the Internet. Both times of day are equally suitable.

The technique itself is quite simple and can be done by anyone. However, it is not necessarily easy for people living in big cities to find good locations for sungazing practice. It's also a bit more difficult in those latitudes that don't get to see the sun very often and where it hides behind clouds.

To cleanse the pineal gland, sungazing should be practiced for nine months as follows:

- Choose sunrise or sunset, according to your needs.

- Find a place, if possible somewhere you can stand barefoot. An ideal location would be by the sea, on a lake, up a mountain, or in a meadow.

- Stand upright there during the first hour of sunrise or during the last hour of sunset. If possible, stand barefoot to get better grounding.

- Blink directly into the sun for only five to ten seconds on the first day.

- Close your eyes and rub your palms together until they grow warm.

- Place the palms of your hands over your closed eyes and look at the afterimage in a relaxed manner until it has disappeared.

- Enjoy the warmth of your palms over your eyes and eye muscles; wait a moment to see if the afterimage appears again.

- Once it has completely disappeared, take your hands away from your eyes, open them, and look around calmly. Don't go away again immediately, but perceive the world with a new look.

- Repeat this on a daily basis for nine months and increase the duration by five to ten seconds each sunny day until you reach a maximum of 45 minutes. If the sky is cloudy, do not add time.

- To maintain the results, run barefoot for 45 minutes each day without looking directly at the sun.

If you have reached 10 minutes of sungazing after 60 days, your vision will improve. When you have reached 15 minutes after 90 days, you are in the best of mental health and feel a peace of mind within you. After 6 months at 30 minutes sungazing, you are free of physical discomfort. After 9 months or 45 minutes of sungazing, your body has turned into a solar reservoir. Your brain is energized.

Hints:

- Even if you cannot sungaze every day, just do it whenever you can. Use sungazing in the morning or evening, regularly or irregularly.

- Increase the duration slowly so as not to damage your eyes - they have to get used to direct sunlight slowly.

- If you can't sungaze at sunrise or sunset, sunbathing is an effective way to recharge your batteries with solar energy at a lighter level. The best time for sunbathing is when the UV index is less than 2. This is usually the case 2 hours after sunrise or before sunset. Avoid sunbathing at other times, except in the winter months when the UV index remains below 2 for a longer period of time. Do not use sunscreen so that your body can naturally perspire the sweat produced by sunbathing.

- In countries with a lot of sun, the whole process takes nine to ten months - in colder regions, it takes a little longer. Be patient!

6.2.6. YOGA

Yoga brings peace to the body and mind. Through yoga, energy is channeled into the mind and thereby increases consciousness. The regular practice of yoga has been proven to increase melatonin production, which in turn leads to an improved sense of well-being.

Swami Sannyasanada of Adelaide University Medical School has demonstrated that the breathing exercises Nadi Shodana (alternating breath) and Tratak (concentration on an object), both techniques from Tantric Yoga, have dramatic effects on melatonin production. They are also good for improving concentration.

Both exercises can be combined, first the alternating breath exercise and then Tratak. Take 20 minutes to do this.

For Tratak, I will first show you a preparatory exercise with a candle to train your concentration. After you have practiced this a few times, you can focus on your third eye instead of a candle.

Besides the mental and spiritual practice, yoga naturally has physical elements that are well-known from the different yoga poses, the so-called asanas. I will show you a yoga pose, Adho Mukha Svanasana, which is best suited for opening the third eye.

6.2.6.1 Nadi Shodana (alternating breath)

- Sit upright on a yoga mat or chair.

- Close your eyes and let your body come to rest.

- Place your right thumb on the right nostril and close it. Place your index and middle finger between your eyebrows.

- Breathe slowly and deeply through the left nostril. Breathing should be silent and harmonious.

- Now close the left nostril with the ring finger, open the right nostril, and breathe out slowly.

- Now breathe in through the right nostril. Then close it with your thumb and exhale through the left nostril.

- You should repeat this procedure for five rounds without a break.

- If you have mastered it well, try a variation where you hold your breath for a while after each inhalation.

- In the next step, inhalation, holding, and exhalation are divided into the ratio 1:4:2; e.g. 5 seconds inhalation, 20 seconds holding, 10 seconds exhalation.

- Repeat this cycle five times also.

6.2.6.2 Tratak with a candle

It is recommended to practice Tratak before going to bed. It helps you to relax and sleep deeply, strengthening the immune system.

- Sit upright on a chair or on the floor and place a candle, eye level, at a distance of 30-40 cm from your eyes.

- Close your eyes and experience your own body by looking inside yourself.

- Draw attention to your breath.

- When you have good contact with your breath, open your eyes and look relaxedly into the flame for 5 to 10 minutes. Look at the uppermost glowing point on the wick and try not to blink.

- Then extinguish the flame, close your eyes, and look at the imprint of light until it subsides and disappears.

At first you will only perceive the flame. Then maybe you will start to think about the blazing of love; that love is something eternal and more than just an impulse or a feeling; something that connects the universe; that love and existence also connect in you. Let your thoughts wander and try to become one with the universe, which is no longer determined by your ego. Develop a firm, basic trust that everything will succeed with the right thoughts.

6.2.6.3 Tratak for the Third Eye

If you have practiced Tratak with a candle a few times, focus on your third eye instead of a candle for your next Tratak meditation:

- Keep your eyes closed and slowly count backwards from 100, number by number, while your attention is focused on your third eye.

- Allow two seconds to pass between each number and the next. Start counting silently in your head: 100 - 99 - 98 - 97 - 96 - 95 .... to 1.

- Sit in an upright position and relax your body.

- Then keep your attention on your third eye for 10 to 15 minutes before refocusing on your surroundings, still keeping your eyes closed.

- Then open your eyes, take three deep breaths in and out, and slowly return to normal.

You may feel a tension or warmth in the area of your third eye. This is not from any headache; it is completely normal and not a cause for concern. It shows you that your third eye is slowly beginning to open. In time, the third eye will open further and soon you will begin to see thoughts, things like in dreams.

By succeeding in turning off the noise in your mind and decelerating the world around you, as if it were standing still, you bring yourself into an inner peace of mind and get a peaceful feeling of love. You know that you are making a difference in the world by facing the chaos in a different way and seeing far beyond.

6.2.6.4 Adho Mukha Svanasana

Adho Mukha Svanasana, the downward facing dog, is a yoga pose that also prepares you to stand on your head and strengthens many brain functions, such as memory, concentration, creative thinking, mental clarity, and the forehead chakra.

But don't worry, you don't need to do a headstand now. Still, the following yoga pose is good preparation for it. If you want, you can approach the headstand later.

This pose is often called "The Yoga Dog" and is one of the most popular yoga exercises. Besides its effects on the brain, this exercise energizes the whole body, is good for back pain, counteracts tension and headaches, and improves blood circulation.

- First, squat with your hands and knees on a yoga mat (dog position). The hands should be placed directly under the shoulders, the elbows stretched, and the knees under the hips.

- Spread your fingers apart and press them into the mat so that the weight is evenly distributed over palms and fingers.

- Breathe out slowly while drawing in your toes and taking your knees off the floor. The legs are put in place, the hips go up, and the bottom moves backwards.

- Even if you feel a strong stretch in your thighs and calves, you should not move your feet forward; leave them where they are.

- To build up the right body tension, push away slightly with your hands so that your heels continue to come down.

- Your arms and elbows should be turned slightly outwards.

- The upper arms and ears should be on one level.

- Relax your head, but do not let it hang down – it should be in line with your back.

- Try holding this pose for about 3 minutes.

- To leave the pose, exhale calmly, bend your knees, bring your feet to your hands, and slowly straighten up vertebra by vertebra.

Note: It is normal for beginners to find that the Achilles tendon is a bit stiff and the arms are weak. With a little practice, you will soon get the hang of it. It is advantageous to have a mirror nearby to control your position.

6.2.7. THIRD EYE KISS

When you kiss someone on the forehead, you know its surprising power. The kiss on the forehead is like kissing the third eye and a person's soul. You will be amazed how this simple act can be so intense and emotional. It is much deeper than most people can realize. Other people do not usually touch our foreheads. We have our hands held, but our foreheads are a bit different. The moment the lips touch our forehead, we feel awakened from within. A kiss stimulated the pineal gland. As the result, melatonin is released. So also a good night kiss has a great impact.

The kiss of the third eye conveys a feeling of security and happiness. Practice this divine touch with your close friends and family. The more often you repeat it, the stronger the feeling and the better the results will be.

6.2.8. HEALING CRYSTALS

Each healing stone has its own aura color, its own vibrations and energy frequencies which are transferred to the person by placing or wearing the stone. By placing a healing stone on a chakra, the vibration of the chakra is stimulated and reactivated. It thus comes into resonance with the stone.

Chakras have their own vibrational frequencies. The color or wavelength of the forehead chakra corresponds to a dark violet (394 nm). To support the third eye in its activity, one should therefore choose a healing stone with a color spectrum from dark blue to dark violet. Suitable crystals for the brow chakra are azurite, amethyst, lapis lazuli, sodalite, and sapphire. They vibrate in a frequency adequate for the forehead chakra. Rock crystal is particularly suitable for bringing the crown chakra, the seat of spirituality and the fusion of mind and soul, into optimal vibration. Its color is white, being transparent with slight violet parts.

The chakras do not lie directly on the skin or the front of the body, but run through the body as an energy axis. A crystal can therefore be placed on both the front and the back of the physical body. You can also just hold a crystal in your hand or wear it around your neck. However, the closer the crystal is to the chakra, the more intense is its effect. Healing stones are also recommended during meditation to accelerate the process of spiritual purification.

6.2.9 ESSENTIAL OILS

Essential oils are extracted from plants and represent the essence or soul of a plant. They support the inner order of body, mind, and soul, promoting their interaction. Their energy frequencies are similar to those of their plant sources and work within different levels of being.

Through their natural energies, essential oils can strengthen the power of the third eye and bring the sixth chakra into the desired balance. They bring greater clarity, objectivity, and wisdom to thoughts, allowing one to see and perceive things better. As you see and perceive things that happen on a higher level of your existence, it raises the spiritual level.

Essential oils help to eliminate imbalances on all levels, be it on the physical level by decalcifying the pineal gland, on the emotional level by eliminating fears, on the mental level in case of difficulties in concentration or abstraction, and especially on the spiritual level. On the spiritual level, imbalances cause - for example - an inability to recognize the truth in its depth, the persistent ignoring of one's own inner voice, or the distrust of one's own intuition.

Before meditating, it is best to rub essential oils on the forehead at the third eye level, either pure or in a mixture of oils. Alternatively, fragrance dispensers can be used.

The following essential oils are best suited to opening the third eye.

Palo Santo Oil

Literally translated it means "holy wood". This oil is obtained from a wild tree found mainly in South America. This tree is traditionally considered mystical and its use dates back to thousands of years of Indian traditions. It is said to have healing powers and the ability to transform negative energies into positive. Its power is associated with the improvement of the third eye. It is used by shamans to increase perception and to purify people, animals, and places. In its native countries, Palo Santo is considered a protective plant that is used to banish negative energy and open the mind for visions in healing ceremonies.

Palo Santo has a rich and sweet aroma with a hint of coconut. It increases spiritual awareness and helps to purify oneself and get into a form of inner prayer. It supports the ability to understand more subtle areas.

Application:

Palo Santo is applied as an oil or by burning Palo Santo wooden sticks:

- Palo Santo Oil: Rub a drop on the forehead before meditation.

- Palo Santo Wood: You can buy it in the form of split fine sticks. The characteristic smell of the resin develops as the sticks burn. To do this, light a stick at the end and let it burn until some embers are produced. You then wave it out and walk through the room and use the smoke to energetically clean it. Afterwards, the stick is placed in a fireproof bowl until it has burned out.

Laurel oil

Laurel wreaths already adorned the heads of kings and emperors who wore them as a sign of victory and glory. The perfection of the ruler was to be transmitted through the laurel wreath as a man exemplary in his thinking and acting.

In Greece, real laurel was used to increase the ability to communicate with God and to understand prophecies and oracles, which means "answer". Laurel was also called "Mantikos", clairvoyant, and is one of the incense ingredients of the oracle mixture of Pythia, the seer of Delphi.

Laurel oil increases consciousness and perception up to clairvoyance and clairaudience. It can also trigger dreams of truth in subtle people.

It has the ability to synchronize the left and right hemispheres of the brain, meaning the thinking mind is connected with the creative mind and the holistic view of things is strengthened. It promotes perception and dreams

Application:

- Mix 1-2 drops of laurel oil with 10 ml of almond oil, put it on the fingertip, and rub it on the forehead at the level of the third eye.

- Fragrance mixture for a fragrance dispenser: Mix one drop each of laurel oil, coriander seed oil, neroli oil, and cedar oil, then put it into the dispenser.

Carrot seed oil

Carrot seed oil has a soul and spiritual stimulating effect. It comes from a plant called Daucus Carota, a plant species of the umbelliferous family.

Carrot seed oil creates harmony between the physical and spiritual areas. It brings light and power to the mind and soul and is therefore recommended for spiritual awakening and enlightenment. It also helps against negative feelings like stress, anger, and rage. It supports a balanced soul life and helps to find your own center. The pleasant scent of carrot stimulates the senses, gives more clarity in the thoughts, and works against fears and confusion.

Application:

- Rub pure carrot seed oil on the forehead before meditation.

- Fragrance dispenser: Mix carrot seed oil with lavender and grapefruit oil; put it in a fragrance dispenser.

Jasmine Oil

Jasmine oil is such a poignant scent that it acts on the soul, inspires imagination and mood, relieves tension, reduces anxiety, increases zest for life and sensuality, boosts self-confidence, increases the positive view of things, creates a connection to the soul, improves intuition, stimulates all the senses, and provides the ability to connect with the entire universe.

Note: Use only genuine essential oil and not synthetic fragrances. You can tell if you have real jasmine oil by the price, because real jasmine oil is very expensive. Synthetic oil smells like jasmine, but has no effect.

Application:

Rub a maximum of one drop of jasmine oil on the forehead at the height of the third eye.

Melissa oil

Melissa oil is considered one of the best essential oils for aromatherapy. Its fresh citrus scent is an excellent antidepressant. Melissa oil has a harmonizing and balancing effect on the nervous system and brings the body, soul, and spirit into harmony.

Melissa oil helps to open the heart chakra and the heart itself for more joy and happiness. It stimulates the pineal gland and the production of serotonin . This makes things that are not commonplace easier to understand. Melissa oil increases intuition, gives access to higher vibrations, and allows you to connect with higher realms by reaching a broader spiritual understanding.

Application:

- Apply a few drops to the forehead or chest.

- In the fragrance dispenser: Combine melissa oil with woody oils and herbal oils.

Chamomile oil

Chamomile oil has a calming effect on the nervous system, removing fears and inner insecurities and bringing the energies back into a flow.

It helps to recognize the influences and impulses of your own ego in order to understand who you really are. It opens the third eye and leads to a higher appreciation. It makes you understand that you are much more than that which is physically and emotionally manifested and shining outwardly.

Your understanding of things is brought to a higher level so that you begin to view your ego-driven behavior from an objective perspective, like a neutral observer from the outside. It helps you to grasp spiritual truths. This, in turn, helps to open your third eye.

Application:

The use of chamomile is versatile. You can apply chamomile oil directly to your forehead, put it in a mixture with woody oils or herbal oils in a fragrance diffuser, use it for massage, or add it to a hot bath.

Rose essence

The genus of the rosaceous plants counts several hundred species of roses. These mainly grow in temperate climates. Since real rose oil is one of the most expensive oils in the world, it is recommended to use rose essence. It is weaker than rose oil, but much stronger than rose water.

Rose essence has a calming, relaxing, and harmonizing effect, gives a feeling of well-being, balances the energy flow, stimulates the mind, and increases intuition. Through its high vibrations, rose essence penetrates the physical and subtle body, bringing them into harmonious alignment, balance, and full of love, compassion, life and mind power, clarity, and creativity.

Rose essences help with spiritual growth processes and provide a special connection to angelic beings who love this fragrance.

Application:

In a fragrance atomizer you can mix rose essences with almost any essential oil.

Clary Sage Oil

Clary sage (Salvia sclarea), also known as nutmeg sage, is an aromatic herb with a spicy fragrance. It is effective against stress and anxiety, enhances creativity, has a euphoric and inspiring effect, revives the mind, stimulates the imagination, and acts as a highly effective antidepressant as it has a positive effect on the mood.

Sage oil is also used for headaches and migraines, autism, epilepsy, and cramps. Due to its antispasmodic properties, it also relieves cramps in the brain and brings the brain to a calm and stable state. This state of calm is necessary for higher explorations and intuitions. For those who frequently suffer from migraines and headaches and want to open their third eye, this essential oil is especially recommended.

Application:

Applied externally to acupressure points or used for massage purposes, clary sage oil has a euphoric effect. Massage into the soles of the feet is particularly effective and increases your energy. With just a few drops you can strengthen your emotional balance and overcome melancholy, fear or anxiety. It can also be used as a bath additive. Add a few drops to a hot bath.

Summary:

Through their natural energies, essential oils can strengthen the power of the third eye and bring the sixth chakra into the desired balance. The effect takes place on all four levels: physical, emotional, mental, and spiritual.

Essential oils are best rubbed on the forehead at the level of the third eye before meditation, either pure or in a mixture of oils. Alternatively, fragrance dispensers are also available.

The following essential oils are recommended:

- Palo Santo oil
- Laurel oil
- Jasmine oil
- Melissa oil
- Chamomile oil
- Rose essence
- Clary Sage oil

6.2.10 MONOATOMIC GOLD

Monoatomic gold (and other monoelements) was known in all Gnostic schools since ancient Egypt. Even initiates like Plato, Aristotle had taken it to expand their consciousness, increase their vibration and activate the full DNA potential.

The Hebrews called it "manna" or the "Bread of God", the Egyptians "Tear from the eye of Horus", the Indians "Vibhuti or bhasma of gold". In alchemy it is considered a substance to transform the human mind and ego with its negative, dense structures into "gold" (the divine soul).

As the name suggests, all monoatomic elements are in a 1-atomic state. Therefore they are free and active, because they are not bound as colloids or metals. There are many different monoatomic elements. Gold plays a central role. It is condensed sunlight and symbolizes our soul state. Most people feel a resonance to gold, and they are automatically attracted to gold because they have the desire to awaken, to become aware of their soul, to live out all their potentials in this earthly world.

The process of awakening can be supported very well with monoatomic gold. It is an all-rounder that can enliven all areas (primary: energetic, emotional, mental and spiritual; secondary: physical), works on existing blockages, dissolves limitations, brings more awareness, strengthens the inner center, promotes the consciousness of love, increases the manifestation power of thoughts, expands perception, breaks up materialism and narrow worldviews, supports self-knowledge, activates the 6th and 7th sense and above all it supports to activate and optimize the pineal gland. It strengthens the soul consciousness and promotes higher potentials and abilities in general. Gold works not only on the chakras, but also on the endocrine glands. It can also strengthen the brain areas.

What can you expect?

Do not expect to take a few drops of monoatomic gold and then be immediately enlightened or have clairvoyant or telepathic abilities. If someone has been living spiritually in darkness for decades and has only limited material consciousness, then a few drops cannot do much, and certainly not at the touch of a button, especially if that person is not yet ready for it.

Ultimately it is up to our consciousness what the monoatomic gold can do for us. If we work mentally in different areas, we can let gold support us.

The big advantage especially with gold is its all-round effect. It affects our consciousness and we can give our wishes and instructions to the monoatomic gold.

Gold is metabolized on a cellular level, it is linked to DNA and can therefore activate or regulate genetic programs. Decisive are our thoughts, our feelings, our beliefs and our spiritual activities, meditations, conscious energy work etc. These are the real influencing factors. The mono elements are only helpers who can support the processes.

The monoatomic gold brings us more soul consciousness. How this affects each person is always different. Consider the gold like a friend with whom you want to achieve something together in teamwork.

On the physical level, monoatomic gold can provide flexibility in our joints, after all, joints are also energetic systems. Many emotions are trapped here, which make us immobile, because our mental-emotional immobility manifests itself in our body. Gold can make us aware of the causes, and ensure that we become more flexible in our consciousness as well as in our body. It also helps with sleep disorders by opening the path to our soul. Excessive energies can be better distributed, tensions disappear, so that the consciousness becomes liberated.

Application:

7 drops in the morning after waking up and 7 drops in the evening at bedtime trickle under the tongue (corresponds to a dosage of 145 micrograms each of monoatomic gold)

If you feel the urge to take more, feel free to do so - but not more than double the dose. After four weeks, I recommend a one to two week break from taking the drops or depending on how you feel.

Summary:

Monoatomic gold has the following effects:

- All-round effects (energetic, emotional, mental, spiritual, physical)
- Activation and optimization of the pineal gland and the third eye
- Strengthening of the heart chakra and increasing the ability to love
- Increase of the suppleness in the joints
- Help with sleep disorders
- Increase of the connection to the soul-being.
- Increase of the perception
- Increase of vitality
- Activation of the lower chakras

Gold is built into those cell structures that have priority for our subconscious. In all processes, mono elements are merely helpers that can strongly support us. To achieve the desired effects, it is important that you actively and consciously pass on your wishes to the monoatomic gold and to be in self-responsibility.

7. HOW TO AVOID CALCIFICATION?

This topic is not easy, especially if you don't live in a wooden hut without Wi-Fi reception in the middle of a forest. It is almost impossible to not be exposed to constant pollution in our current "civilized" world, like through electrosmog, food, our everyday life, and our working life.

But even if you can't prevent all pollution, there are still some things you can do - even if it doesn't happen overnight.

Here are some suggestions:

- Abstain from fluorides as far as possible, but also from tobacco, alcohol, milk, sugar, finished products, and meat. Change your diet to alkaline in order to not over-acidify your body.

- Meditate regularly. Meditating for half an hour before sleeping is highly recommended. Support the meditation with one of the presented methods like sounds, healing stones, or essential oils.

- Avoid stress and gloomy thoughts.

- Cleanse the pineal gland of fluorides through the combination of numbers shown. Support the cleansing, for example, with micro algae like AFA-algae or chlorella algae.

- If you have the opportunity, practice sungazing.

- Drink good spring water regularly to eliminate toxins quickly.

- As tap water in many countries is infested with fluoride (in the UK, at least), it is advisable to use a filtered shower head/tap/etc. for showers and baths, as you absorb a lot of water through the skin

- Bring yourself into a state of joy again and again.

- Fantasize consciously and imagine your personal paradise, what you think it should look like in this world, and as if it had already happened. From quantum physics we know that thoughts or feelings create reality.

- Do creative activities like painting, making music, photography, etcetera.

- Minimize your daily radiation exposure. Keep your sleeping place free of Wi-Fi, cell phone radiation, and electronic devices; switch off routers, DECT phones, and multiple sockets at night.

Tip: The British engineer and sound healer Simon Fox developed a device years ago to strengthen the body's own biofield or EMF defense system and increase immunity to Wi-Fi radiation. This makes you more immune to electrosmog from various sources, regardless of whether it is generated by cell phone masts, DECT phones, high-frequency pollution in the power grid, or Bluetooth. It is distributed by his company Resonancesciences.uk (formerly known as Calmspace Pro). The German company Vivobase.de, whose devices are also based on the activation of the natural protective shield, is taking a similar path.

- Go to bed at 10 pm at the latest so that the pineal gland can produce melatonin.

- Before you have another vaccination, ask for the package insert of the ingredient with the respective components. Mercury should not be included.

- Do not hold your smartphone directly against your head. Even Nokia recommends a distance of at least one meter. Use either a hands-free car kit or a "healthy" headset that does not conduct the electrosmog from your phone directly into your ear.

Tip: The Airtube headsets are especially recommended. They are not much more expensive than standard Bluetooth headsets, but they reduce the HF radiation by up to 99%. They work with iPhones, Samsung Galaxy, and other smartphones.

8. WHAT HAPPENS WHEN YOU WAKE UP?

Through the forehead chakra or third eye, we have access to the so-called Akasha wisdom ('Akasha', Sanskrit; means space or ether), a knowledge that encompasses everything that has ever existed. It provides access to the universe.

When your pineal gland is cleansed and activated, your spiritual being awakens. This also means stepping into a feeling of love, a feeling of consciousness, and the passion of compassion and pity.

You will understand the truth - understand that all people in this universe consist of one person and that we are all a part, a being from one and the same family. As the divisive elements dissolve, you will banish spiritual and visionary negativity from your life.

In concrete terms, this means for the spiritual realm:

- that your perception is sharpened and you start to look "beyond your own nose". When you are with people, you stop judging them. You see things for what they are, directly and unadulterated, without interpreting them with your mind. You simply allow things to be as they are without judging them and feel a sense of connection with everything. The moment it happens, you know it is happening.

- You recognize interactions from outside, as if you were looking at them from further away. This results in a certain far-sightedness which is also called clairvoyance or clairsentience.

- You have the feeling of being protected and that you are embedded in a larger cosmic event.

- You live more in the here and now, instead of within a self-imposed time pattern. This sharpens your awareness and mindfulness.

- You realize how important and significant you are, as well as all of your thoughts, feelings, and actions, because you feel your own effect in everything.

- The most obvious signal of the opening of the third eye is when your foresight and intuition increases. Intuition is the ability to know that something could happen before it happens. You instinctively know whether something is right or wrong without your logical mind judging the situation. You notice that another instance is added, namely the instance of awareness, which makes you look at and judge the situation as if from the outside. This feeling becomes stronger over time, eventually acting as a guiding process in your daily life. You begin to intuitively feel warning signs and know what your next action should be – and you recognize manipulations and subliminal messages.

- You will also notice changes on the psychological level, such as spontaneous feelings of happiness and euphoria, a higher memory performance, more joy in life, the decrease of depression, higher creativity and imagination, and a better ability to concentrate.

CONCLUSION

The pineal gland is one of the most important organs in the human body. It is our soul organ, the gate to our freedom. In addition to its important task of producing melatonin, which has been proven to have a highly positive influence on the aging process ("undermortality hormone"), it is responsible for the abilities of the 4th dimension through the production of DMT, our body's own neurotransmitter. This includes all forms of expansion of consciousness such as clairvoyance, clairaudience, clairsentience, telepathy, higher intuition, and much more. Only these two substances provide the basis for the development of a higher consciousness.

The problem many people have at present is that their pineal gland is not actively working because it is calcified or blocked. This is caused by life-shortening foods that poison the intestines, by the poisoning of the brain via fluorides, pesticides, and mercury, by the manipulative effects of the media, and by electrosmog with torsion fields that turn in exactly the opposite direction to our natural fields, therefore making us ill.

Due to daily stress and (survival) fears, most people are also kept in the low vibrational areas, i.e. in the lower chakras, which have to do with survival, sexuality, food, and ego. Thus, they have little time, leisure, and interest to deal with their spiritual development.

Without a cleaned and activated pineal gland, however, medial abilities cannot be awakened. Only when the pineal gland is intact - and free from blockages and all these things - can it do wonderful things and open the third eye.

So, if you do something for yourself you should become active. No longer put your power in the hands of other forces, whoever or whatever they may be. In fact, you are much stronger and more powerful than you might think.

In this book I have shown you a variety of ways to cleanse your pineal gland and avoid future calcification. One of the most effective methods works through the mind. Our mind is above matter; that is why meditation is so essential to truly progress and find the divine soul that you are.

I wish you good luck and success on your path!

Finally, if you enjoyed this book, then I'd like to ask you for a favor, would you be kind enough to leave a review for this book on Amazon? It'd be greatly appreciated!

If you did not like the book or if you have suggestions for improvement, please send me an e-mail.

Thank you!

Anna Mai

PHOTOS

https://www.bigstockphoto.com Copyright:

- Peter Hermes Furian, Stockfoto-ID: 128843801, Chakras

- Nikki Zalewski, Stockfoto-ID: 149581028, Crystal ball surrounded by healing crystals

- tomozina, Stockfoto-ID: 181209445, Neon sound line. Vector illustration.

- deosum, Stockfoto-ID: 83641898, Illustration of human aura

- udaix, Stockfoto-ID: 168855311, Median Section of Human Brain Anatomical structure

- fizkes, Stockfoto-ID: 85838699, Vishnu Mudra

- fizkes, Stockfoto-ID: 85430927, Sporty girl on white background stretching in downward-facing dog yoga

- Yellowj, Stockfoto-ID: 12513959, yoga woman on green grass

- Maridav, Stockfoto-ID: 86028956, Zen yoga woman doing meditation

- Maridav, Stockfoto-ID: 155300765, Happy woman feeling free with open arms in sunshine at beach sunset.

- An Vino, Stockfoto-ID: 127802543, Yoga is a set of different spiritual, mental physical practices beautiful card

- Swill Klitch, Stockfoto-ID: 128491493, Retro wave shiny head silhouette over neon landscape

IMPRINT

Anna Mai (author and editor)

c/o Papyrus Autoren-Club

Pettenkoferstr. 16-18

10247 Berlin / Germany

annamai@ereadmedia.com

The information herein is offered for informational purposes solely, and is universal as so. The presentation of the information is without contract or any type of guarantee assurance.

The trademarks that are used are without any consent, and the publication of the trademark is without permission or backing by the trademark owner. All trademarks and brands within this book are for clarifying purposes only and are the owned by the owners themselves, not affiliated with this document.

Made in the USA
Las Vegas, NV
13 March 2021